The Industrial Revolution

———

工业革命

Chinese-English Introduction of the Industrial Revolution for Children

中英双语给孩子讲工业革命

小机器大进步

SMALL MACHINES BIG PROGRESS

懿海文化——著/绘 **刘丽丽**——译

科学普及出版社

·北 京·

CONTENTS

目 录

工业革命
The Industrial Revolution

　　18世纪至19世纪初，工业革命首先在英国爆发，随后席卷了欧洲其他地区。以工业化批量制造为主导的经济取代了以手工劳动为基础的经济，生产和贸易也随之急剧增加。在工业化的影响下，欧洲国家的社会结构发生了根本性变化。

In the 18th century to the early 19th century, the Industrial Revolution first erupted in Britain and then swept across other regions of Europe. An economy dominated by industrialized mass production replaced the labor-based economy, and production and trade increased sharply. Under the influence of industrialization, the social structure of European countries underwent fundamental changes.

燃料的开发与利用
DEVELOPMENT AND UTILIZATION OF FUELS

为了找到一种可以用于照明的燃料，人们开始对石油衍生物进行研究，并最终用它取代了煤炭。

In order to find a fuel that could be used for lighting, people began to study petroleum derivatives and eventually replaced coal with it.

你知道吗?

DID YOU KNOW?

工业革命期间，工人每天的工作时间长达 **14**小时。

During the Industrial Revolution, workers had to work up to 14 hours a day.

泰勒主义 TAYLORISM

泰勒主义的原理包括：

使用科学方法工作，而不是工人的"经验之谈"；

评估工人在特定工作中的能力，并指导他们发挥最佳水平；

评估工人的效率，并在必要时提供额外的指导；

管理者负责计划和培训，工人根据培训的内容进行工作。

The principles of Taylorism include:
Work using science, not just workers' guesses;
Assess workers' abilities for specific jobs and guide them to do their best;
Check how well workers are doing and give extra guidance if needed;
Managers plan and train, workers follow the training for their jobs.

弗雷德里克·泰勒 FREDERICK TAYLOR

是一名美国工程师，他创立了一套有效利用人力资源的体系。

He was an American engineer who created a system for optimizing human resources.

流水线作业 ASSEMBLY LINE

对工业生产来说，生产线或生产链是一种巨大的变革。它的基础是流水作业，就是通过给每个工人委派日渐复杂的机械设备的特定专业职能来组织生产。这不仅节省了成本，还显著提高了产量。

For industrial production, the assembly line or production chain was a huge change. Its foundation was the concept of the assembly line, which organized production by assigning specific tasks to each worker for increasingly complex machinery. This not only saved costs, but also significantly increased production output.

人口爆炸 POPULATION BOOM

这一时期，欧洲人口急剧增加。1850年，人口数量已经达到2.66亿。

During this period, the population of Europe increased rapidly. By 1850, the population had reached 266 million.

蒸汽机 STEAM ENGINE

蒸汽机的发明促进了机械生产及铁路和轮船等运输方式的发展。

The invention of the steam engine promoted the development of machinery, as well as transportation methods such as railways and steamships.

珍妮纺纱机 SPINNING JENNY

珍妮纺纱机发明于1764年，对英国纺织工业的发展起到了举足轻重的作用。

The invention of the spinning Jenny in 1764 played a crucial role in the development of the British textile industry.

工厂的诞生
The Birth of the Factory

家庭或手工作坊的组织模式被工厂这种新型组织模式取代，拥有工厂的纺织工业成了工业革命时期的支柱产业之一。

The organization model of home or craft workshops was replaced by the new model of factories, and the textile industry with factories became one of the pillar industries of the Industrial Revolution.

工人 WORKERS

做工的人有男人、女人和孩子，工人阶级诞生。

Men, women, and children worked in factories, giving rise to the working class.

绕线机 WINDING MACHINES

纺纱机 SPINNERS

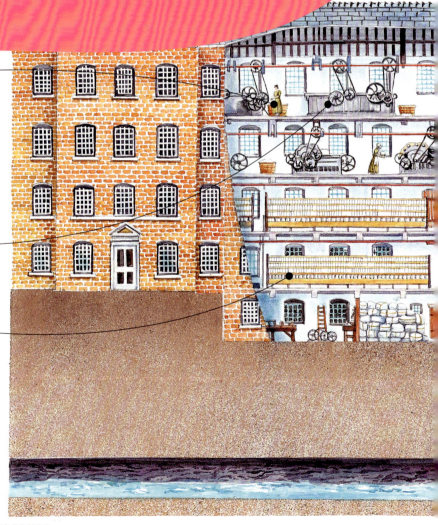

组织化 ORGANIZATION

纺织业是第一个在工厂组织生产的行业。在这种组织模式下，每个工人只负责产品生产的一部分，以提高生产效率。为了达到这个目的，工人和机器需要处在同一个厂房内，并且每项特定的生产任务要在不同的厂房区域来完成。

The textile industry was the first industry to organize production in factories. In this organizational model, each worker was responsible for only one part of the product to improve production efficiency. To achieve this goal, workers and machines needed to be in the same factory building, and each specific production task had to be completed in different areas of the factory.

梳棉机
CARDING MACHINES

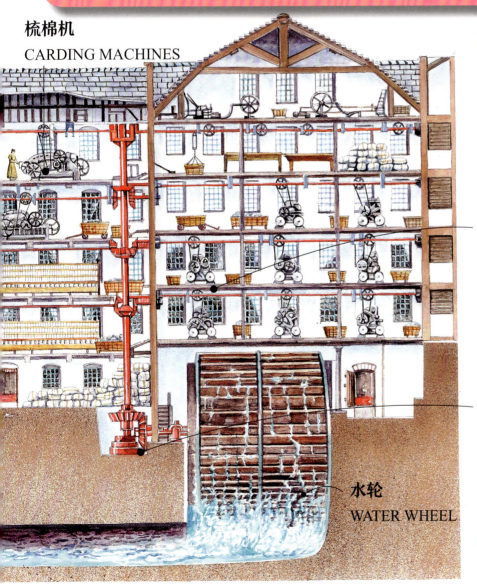

水轮
WATER WHEEL

照明 LIGHTING

1805年前后，煤气灯问世，工人的工作时间得以延长。

Around 1805, gas lamps were invented, which allowed workers to extend their working hours.

工作区域
WORKING AREAS

不同的生产任务在不同的工作区域完成。

Each different task occupied a different area.

水能的应用
HYDRAULIC ENERGY UTILIZATION

通过传动轴，水能被传输到工厂的各个区域。

Water power was transmitted to different areas of the factory through transmission shafts.

直到1880年，**自行车**才开始投入大规模生产。

It wasn't until 1880 that bicycles began to be produced on a large scale.

飞梭 FLYING SHUTTLE

飞梭是纺织行业的第一项发明。

飞梭依靠在滑轨上移动的轮子，将线从一端穿到另一端。

有了飞梭之后，织出来的布更宽了，织布速度也大大加快。

用手工梭子织布时，布料的宽度受限于织布工人手臂的伸展幅度。

The flying shuttle was the first invention in the textile industry.
By moving wheels along a sliding track, the flying shuttle passed the thread from one end to the other.
With the invention of the flying shuttle, the cloth became wider and the weaving speed was greatly increased.
When fabric was woven using a manual shuttle, the width of the fabric depended on the reach of the weaver's arms.

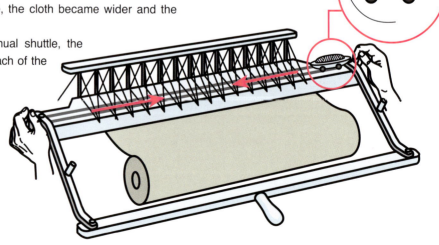

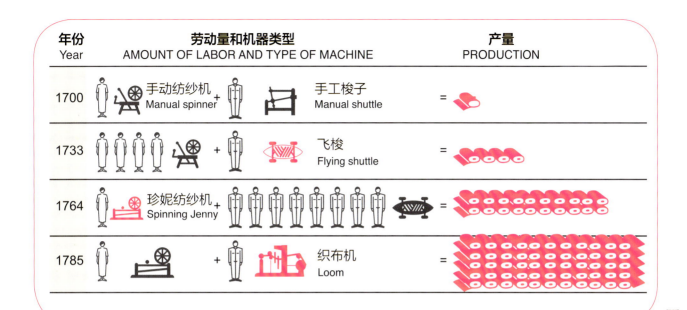

年份 Year	劳动量和机器类型 AMOUNT OF LABOR AND TYPE OF MACHINE	产量 PRODUCTION
1700	手动纺纱机 Manual spinner + 手工梭子 Manual shuttle	=
1733	+ 飞梭 Flying shuttle	=
1764	珍妮纺纱机 Spinning Jenny +	=
1785	+ 织布机 Loom	=

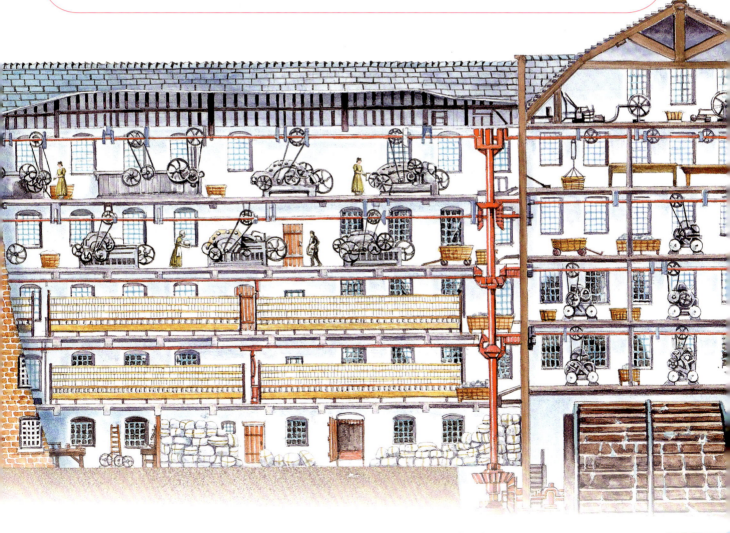

工厂工人
Industrial Workers

　　第一批工厂工人来自英国的纺织工业。他们原本是城市或农村的工匠或农民，纺织业的兴起让他们得以走出家门，开始在外工作。雇主给他们提供工具和原材料，作为交换，他们领取工资，但工资十分微薄。

The first generation of industrial workers came from the textile industry in Britain. They were originally artisans or farmers in urban or rural areas, and the rise of the textile industry allowed them to leave their homes and start working outside. Employers provided them with tools and raw materials, and in exchange, they received wages, but the wages were meager.

生产率 PRODUCTIVITY

蒸汽机的使用降低了生产成本，提高了生产率。

The use of steam engines reduced costs and increased productivity.

纪律 DISCIPLINE

工头负责监督工人们的工作。

The foremen were responsible for overseeing the work of the workers.

蒸汽机 STEAM ENGINE

詹姆斯·瓦特对蒸汽机进行了革命性改进。

蒸汽机是新技术发展的推动力，也是纺织工业和冶金工业的动力来源。

James Watt made revolutionary improvements to the steam engine.
The steam engine was a driving force behind the development of new technology and a source of power for the textile and metallurgical industries.

所有者 OWNERS

只有商人才能买得起庞大而昂贵的机器，并将其安置在工厂里。

As the machines were expensive and huge, only businessmen could afford them and install them in factories.

棉花 COTTON

来自英国的殖民地，是非常廉价的原材料，极易供销给海外市场。

Cotton from British colonies was a very cheap raw material and was easily supplied to overseas markets.

差异性 DIFFERENCES

虽然男性工人和女性工人做着相同的工作，但他们得到的工资不一样。

Although male and female did the same jobs, they were paid differently.

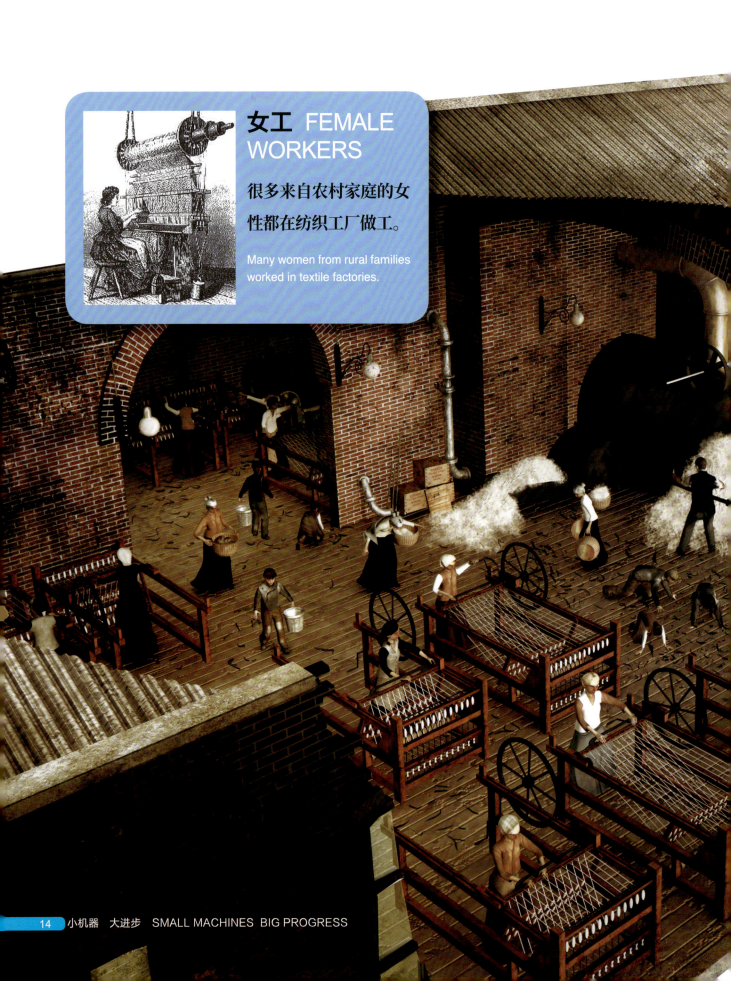

女工 FEMALE WORKERS

很多来自农村家庭的女性都在纺织工厂做工。

Many women from rural families worked in textile factories.

演变 EVOLUTION

在短短几年内，纺织制造业就从手工生产变成了机械化生产行业。关键时间点如下：

In just a few years, textile manufacturing went from manual production to mechanized production. The key timeline is as follows:

1788

蒸汽动力织布机问世。第一家使用这种系统的纺织工厂在英国应运而生。因为不再依赖水力，工厂也搬离了河边。

The steam-powered loom was invented. The first textile factory to use this system emerged in Britain. Because it no longer relied on water power, the factory moved away from the riverbank.

1794

伊莱·惠特尼发明了可快速去除棉籽的轧棉机并获得专利权，大大降低了棉花的加工成本，并由此带动了人们对棉布的需求。

Eli Whitney invented the cotton gin, which quickly removed cotton seeds and obtained a patent. This greatly reduced the processing cost of cotton and stimulated people's demand for cotton cloth.

1801

法国的约瑟夫·玛丽·雅卡尔发明了打洞卡片系统，开启了机械自动编织图案的先河。

Joseph Marie Jacquard of France invented the punch card system, which opened the door to mechanically automated weaving patterns.

1830

第一台缝纫机获得专利。

The first sewing machine was patented.

煤矿
Coal Mines

　　随着工业革命的发展，新型的蒸汽动力驱动的机器对煤炭的需求急剧上升。为了满足这一需求，地下矿井的数量迅速增加，矿工们不得不忍受恶劣的环境，前往越来越深的地下挖煤。

As the Industrial Revolution continued to advance, the demand for coal sharply increased due to new steam-powered machines. To meet this demand, the number of underground mines rapidly increased, and miners had to endure harsh environments and dig deeper and deeper underground to extract coal.

童工 CHILD LABOR

他们能够钻过狭窄的坑道，所得的工资比成年人低。

They were able to crawl through narrow tunnels. But they earned lower wages than adults.

暗无天日的工作 A DARK JOB

矿工的主要工作就是钻岩取矿。然而，除了这些，他们还要搭建木质支架，用以支撑坑道，防止坍塌；同时还要铺设运送材料的轨道，并把矿物装到小货车上，从井下运送到地面。

The main job of a miner was to drill and extract minerals from rocks. However, in addition to this, they also had to build wooden supports to prop up the tunnels and prevent collapse. They also laid tracks for transporting materials and loaded the minerals onto small carts to be transported from underground to the surface.

装运
LOAD AND TRANSPORT

矿物被装车运到地面。

The mineral was brought to the ground.

工具 TOOL

需要使用镐和锹。

Pickaxes and shovels were needed.

掘井采矿
EXTRACTION SHAFTS

掘井采矿时，矿工的姿势和动作受限，相当不舒服。为了寻找矿层，他们常常需要弯着腰走上很长的距离。

When working, miners had limited postures and movements, which could be quite uncomfortable. In order to search for mineral veins, they often had to walk long distances while bending over.

地面建筑
ON THE SURFACE

管理部门
MANAGEMENT

绳索
ROPES

巷道
GALLERIES

矿洞楼层
COAL SEAM

运输
TRANSPORT

地面建筑 ON THE SURFACE

他们修建了木质建筑物来保护矿井的入口。

Wooden structures were built to protect the entrances of the mine shafts.

管理部门 MANAGEMENT

这里是管理层员工的办公室，也是发出工作指令的地方。

These structures served as offices for the management staff and were used to issue work orders.

绳索 ROPES

矿物和工具的运送都是通过一口竖井完成的。

The transportation of minerals and tools was accomplished through a vertical shaft.

巷道 GALLERIES

井筒、巷道、硐室以及通风管道都是采矿所需的重要构造。

The shafts,galleries,chambers,and ventilation ducts were all important structures needed for mining.

矿洞楼层 COAL SEAM

地下通道由一级级的木质台阶相连接。

The underground passages were connected by a series of wooden steps.

运输 TRANSPORT

矿物由行驶在轨道上的小货车运输。

The minerals were transported by small carts running on tracks.

工业资本主义
Industrial Capitalism

工业革命带来了经济的巨大增长，贸易和通信开始国际化。在这种背景下，19世纪下半叶，以自由贸易为基础的工业资本主义得到了飞速发展。

The Industrial Revolution brought about tremendous economic growth, and trade and communication began to internationalize. In this context, in the second half of the 19th century, industrial capitalism based on free trade saw rapid development.

银行业的发展
THE DEVELOPMENT OF BANKING INDUSTRY

工业革命和国际贸易的发展不仅促成了新银行的诞生，而且使银行服务项目变得多样化。18—19世纪，作为海上强权的英国一直控制着国际贸易，也因此带动银行业不断发展壮大。

The development of the Industrial Revolution and international trade not only led to the birth of new banks, but also diversified banking services. Between the 18th and 19th centuries, as a maritime power, the United Kingdom controlled international trade, which in turn drove the continuous growth and expansion of the banking industry.

股份和股票交易 SHARES AND STOCK TRADING

对新机器的投资需求，促使公司通过出售股份来鼓励投资，由此使股票市场得到进一步强化和发展。

The demand for investment in new machinery prompted companies to encourage investment by selling shares, which in turn further strengthened and developed the stock market.

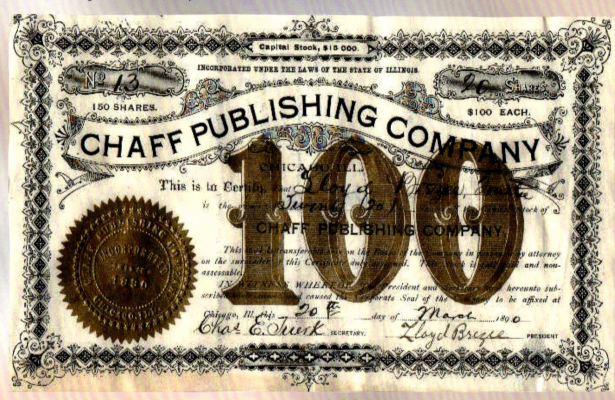

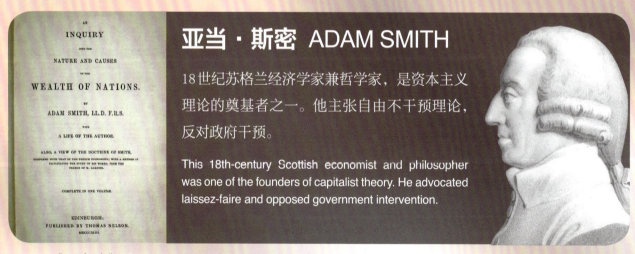

《国富论》

亚当·斯密 ADAM SMITH

18世纪苏格兰经济学家兼哲学家，是资本主义理论的奠基者之一。他主张自由不干预理论，反对政府干预。

This 18th-century Scottish economist and philosopher was one of the founders of capitalist theory. He advocated laissez-faire and opposed government intervention.

殖民地 COLONIES

为了寻找更多的原料和开拓新的市场，欧洲殖民主义应运而生。

In order to find more raw materials and explore new markets, European colonialism emerged.

银行 BANKS

大规模的工业生产带动资本在国际范围内流动，而银行则成了这一新型经济体系的支柱。

The large-scale industrial production drove the flow of capital on an international scale, with banks becoming the backbone of this new economic system.

万国邮政联盟 THE UNIVERSAL POSTAL UNION

高效的信息交流对国际贸易的发展至关重要。铁路网和航线不断扩张，电报也得到进一步发展。为了协调国际邮政事务，万国邮政联盟得以成立。

Effective communication was crucial for the development of international trade. The expansion of railway networks and shipping routes, as well as the further development of telegraphs, facilitated the process. To coordinate international postal affairs, the Universal Postal Union was established.

社会运动
Social Movement

  随着工业的发展，一个由领薪水的工人组成的新社会阶层出现了，即无产阶级或工人阶级，进而引发了各种社会和文化变革。受农业危机和新工作机会的驱动，很多农民涌进了大城市，结果却发现自己处于一个被剥削和被压榨的体系之下。他们的不满和抱怨为工会和政党的建立奠定了基础。

With the development of industry, a new social class composed of waged workers emerged, namely the proletariat or working class, which led to various social and cultural changes. Driven by agricultural crises and new job opportunities, many farmers flocked to large cities, only to find themselves in a system of exploitation and oppression. Their dissatisfaction and complaints laid the foundation for the establishment of labor unions and political parties.

现代化的萌芽
THE EMERGENCE OF MODERNIZATION

对第一代产业工人来说，要适应严苛而陌生的体系并不容易。劳动权的缺乏意味着每个工厂都有不同的工作体制。渐渐地，工人们开始要求改善工作条件，这是第一个社会主义者和无政府主义者工会的起源。他们利用罢工和联合抵制的手段，要求提高工资待遇、获取平等权利和减少工作时间。

It was not easy for the first-generation industrial workers to adapt to the harsh and unfamiliar system. The lack of labor rights meant that each factory had a different work system. Gradually, workers began to demand improved working conditions, giving rise to the first socialist and anarchist labor unions. They used strikes and boycotts to demand better wages, equal rights, and to reduce working hours.

宪章运动
CHARTISM

宪章运动是指发生在19世纪30年代和40年代的英国工人运动，其目标是通过争取普选权和其他政治改革来解决工人阶级的社会和经济问题。

Chartism refers to the worker movement that took place in the 1830s and 1840s in Britain, with the goal of addressing the social and economic issues faced by the working class through the pursuit of universal suffrage and other political reforms.

五一国际劳动节 MAY DAY

1886年5月1日，美国爆发了大规模的罢工运动，即历史上著名的"芝加哥干草市场惨案"，其目的是实行8小时工作制。结果，运动遭到了政府的残酷镇压，其中四名参与者被处以绞刑。这一事件成为五一国际劳动节的起源。

On May 1, 1886, a large-scale strike broke out in the United States, known as the "Haymarket affair" in Chicago, with the aim of implementing an 8-hour workday. As a result, the movement was brutally suppressed by the government, and four participants were sentenced to death by hanging. This event became the origin of International Workers' Day, also known as May Day.

《共产党宣言》
COMMUNIST MANIFESTO

卡尔·马克思，德国著名哲学家、历史学家、社会学家、经济学家、作家与思想家。他的杰作《共产党宣言》首次出版于1848年，是历史上最具影响力的政治纲领之一。恩格斯是他学术研究的资助者和合作者。

Karl Marx, a renowned German philosopher, historian, sociologist, economist, writer, and thinker, wrote the masterpiece *The Communist Manifesto*, first published in 1848, which is one of the most influential political manifestos in history. Engels was his financial supporter and collaborator in his academic research.

基本家庭
The Basic Family

工业革命造成大批人口从农村向城市迁移，于是亲人间的情感变得越来越淡薄，家庭成员的数目也变得越来越少。这就是核心家庭或现代西方家庭的起源，这种家庭由父母及其未婚子女组成。在工业化过程中，家庭与工作场所逐渐发生分离，从而使公共场所和私人领域之间出现了明显的界限。

The Industrial Revolution led to a large number of people moving from rural areas to cities, which caused emotional bonds between family members to become weaker, and the number of family members to become smaller. This was the origin of the nuclear family or modern Western family, which consists of parents and their unmarried children. During the process of industrialization, the family gradually became separated from the workplace, resulting in a clear boundary between public spaces and private domains.

被法律遗弃 ABANDONED

就业保障法的缺失，使得弱势群体更易受到压迫和剥削。

The absence of employment protection laws made vulnerable groups more susceptible to oppression and exploitation.

儿童 THE CHILDREN

随着女性不断走出家庭，参与工作，原有的家庭生活模式受到影响。有时候，母亲们不得不狠心抛下各自的孩子，让他们互相照顾。

As women increasingly stepped out of their homes to participate in the workforce, the traditional family life patterns were impacted. At times, mothers had to make the heart-wrenching decision to leave their children behind.

财产 BELONGINGS

第一批工人阶级家庭的财产少得可怜。除了衣服和个人卫生用品，他们唯一拥有的就是自己。

The first batch of working-class families had very little property. Apart from clothes and personal hygiene items, the only thing they owned was themselves.

父亲 THE FATHER

男人们开始外出工作，他们是家庭的主要经济支柱。

Men began to work outside of the house as the primary breadwinners for their families.

母亲 THE MOTHER

不外出工作的母亲会担起提供精神支持及照料家庭的责任。

Mothers who did not work outside of the house would take on the responsibility of providing emotional support and caring for the household.

哺育后代 NURTURING OFFSPRING

生小孩意味着失去工作，那时候根本就没有产假这种说法。

Having children meant losing their jobs, and there was no such thing as maternity leave back then.

改变习惯 CHANGING HABITS

刚刚搬到城市的农村家庭不得不学会适应陌生的环境和习惯，其生活方式也由此发生了天翻地覆的变化——家庭不再是一个生产单位，家庭生活的维持依赖于每一位家庭成员的工作。工资少之又少，为了生存，所有家庭成员都必须找到一份工作。

Rural families who had just moved to the city had to learn to adapt to unfamiliar environments and customs, and their way of life underwent a dramatic change. The family was no longer a production unit, and the maintenance of family life depended on the work of each family member. Wages were extremely low, and in order to survive, every family member had to find a job.

被无视的童年
CHILDHOOD NEGLECTED

工业化使人们开始把童年视作人生中一个特殊的成长阶段。在工业化早期，孩子们常常受到工厂主的剥削，他们做着成人的工作，工资却比成人低得多。

Industrialization made people begin to see childhood as a special stage of human growth. In the early stages of industrialization, children were often exploited by factory owners. They did adult work but were paid much less than adults.

适应城市生活 ADAPTING TO URBAN LIFE

从农村生活到城市生活的转变是一个非常艰难的过程。许多女性仍然保留着原有的习惯，经常跑到市区附近的河边洗衣服。

The transition from rural to urban life was a very difficult process. Many women retained their traditional habits of washing clothes by the riverside near the city center.

现代城市
Modern Cities

工业革命促使农民加入工业大军，为城市带来了翻天覆地的变化。为了适应新的时代，城市必须进行改建。于是，许多宽阔的街道、公园、花园以及新的交通系统纷纷出现。

The Industrial Revolution led to the influx of farmers into the industrial workforce, bringing about tremendous changes to the city. To adapt to the new era, the city had to undergo renovation. As a result, many broad streets, parks, gardens, and new transportation systems emerged.

巴黎 PARIS

19世纪下半叶，法国首都彻底重建，成为世界大都市的典范。奥斯曼男爵便是这项大改造工程的负责人。

In the second half of the 19th century, the French capital was completely rebuilt and became a model of a world metropolis. Baron Haussmann was the person in charge of this major renovation project.

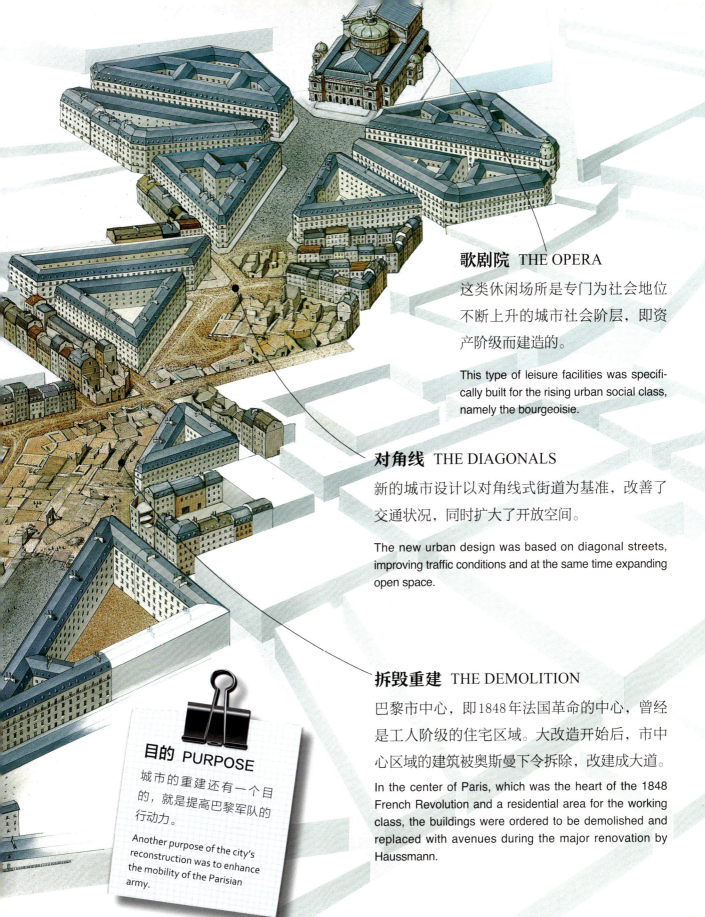

歌剧院 THE OPERA

这类休闲场所是专门为社会地位不断上升的城市社会阶层，即资产阶级而建造的。

This type of leisure facilities was specifically built for the rising urban social class, namely the bourgeoisie.

对角线 THE DIAGONALS

新的城市设计以对角线式街道为基准，改善了交通状况，同时扩大了开放空间。

The new urban design was based on diagonal streets, improving traffic conditions and at the same time expanding open space.

拆毁重建 THE DEMOLITION

巴黎市中心，即1848年法国革命的中心，曾经是工人阶级的住宅区域。大改造开始后，市中心区域的建筑被奥斯曼下令拆除，改建成大道。

In the center of Paris, which was the heart of the 1848 French Revolution and a residential area for the working class, the buildings were ordered to be demolished and replaced with avenues during the major renovation by Haussmann.

目的 PURPOSE

城市的重建还有一个目的，就是提高巴黎军队的行动力。

Another purpose of the city's reconstruction was to enhance the mobility of the Parisian army.

你知道吗？
DID YOU KNOW?

巴黎改建后，在收回的土地上一共建造了 **74 000** 栋商店和豪华住宅。

After the rebuilding of Paris, a total of 74,000 shops and luxury residences were built on the reclaimed land.

奥斯曼男爵
BARON HAUSSMANN

奥斯曼男爵曾任塞纳省省长（1853—1870），负责巴黎的改建工程。他拆除了旧的工人阶级住宅区，将其改建成宽阔的林荫大道、公园和花园等，使巴黎成为法兰西第二帝国耀眼的新都。

Baron Haussmann served as the prefect of the Seine department (1853-1870) and was responsible for the reconstruction of Paris. He demolished the old working-class residential areas and rebuilt them into wide boulevards, parks, and gardens, making Paris a dazzling new capital of the Second French Empire.

新城市规划目标
THE NEW URBAN PLANNING GOAL

奥斯曼男爵以两条垂直的轴线为基准对巴黎进行了改建：一条南北走向（圣米歇尔大道和塞瓦斯托波尔大道），另一条东西走向（里沃利路）。两条干道在沙特莱广场交汇。这样一来，不仅车辆和行人的流量能得到有效控制，执法力量的调动也更为迅速和便捷。

The new urban planning goal was to use two perpendicular axes as the basis for the reconstruction of Paris by Baron Haussmann: one running north-south (Boulevard Saint-Michel and Boulevard de Sébastopol) and the other running east-west (Rue de Rivoli). The two main thoroughfares intersected at the Place du Châtelet. This arrangement not only effectively controlled traffic and pedestrian flow, but also allowed for the rapid and convenient deployment of law enforcement personnel.

- 老城区 Historic center
- 新区 New districts
- 新公园 New parks
- 城墙 Walls
- 老街 Old streets
- 新大道 New avenues and boulevards

曼彻斯特
Manchester

工业革命时期，技术与科学的创新层出不穷，带动了英国许多城市的发展。建筑学的地位在几个世纪以来首次受到质疑：比起建筑师的艺术技巧，工程师的技能似乎更加契合技术创新的需要。这意味着机械化时代的到来。曼彻斯特是第一个工业化城市，它发展得实在太快了，许多社会问题随之出现。

During the Industrial Revolution, there were numerous technological and scientific innovations which drove the development of many cities in Britain. The status of architecture was questioned for the first time in centuries: engineering skills seemed more aligned with technological innovation need than the artistic skills of architects. This heralded the arrival of the mechanized age. Manchester was the first industrialized city and it developed at an incredibly fast pace, but it also brought about many social problems.

双面曼彻斯特 DUAL MANCHESTER

1760—1830年，曼彻斯特的人口从1.7万激增到18万，城市也在同步发展。然而，资产阶级和无产阶级的居住区却呈现出明显的差异。前者拥有舒适的生活环境和服务设施，而后者的住房则建在工厂附近，杂乱无章。

During the period of 1760-1830, Manchester's population skyrocketed from 17, 000 to 180, 000, and the city developed accordingly. However, there was a clear distinction between the living areas of the bourgeoisie and the proletariat. The former had comfortable living environments and service facilities, while the latter's housing was built near factories and was disorderly and chaotic.

位置 LOCATION

许多河流和运河流经曼彻斯特。随着城市的工业化，货物的运输量也大幅增加。

Many rivers and canals flow through Manchester. With the industrialization of the city, the volume of goods transportation also increased significantly.

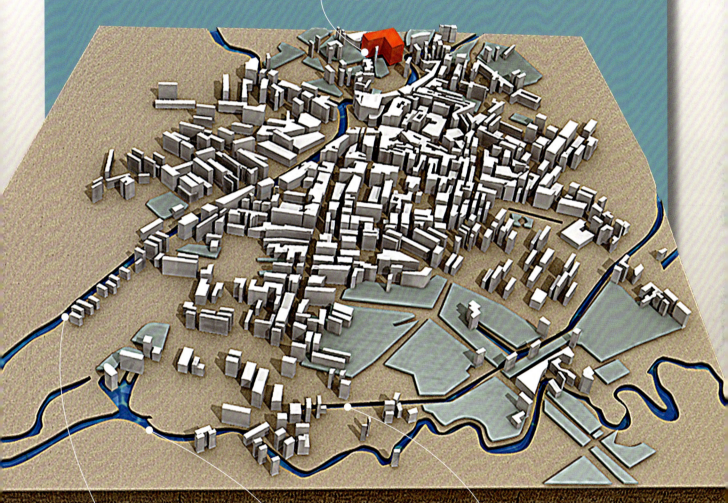

维多利亚站
VICTORIA STATION

艾威尔河
RIVER IRWELL

布里奇沃特运河
BRIDGEWATER CANAL

罗奇代尔运河
ROCHDALE CANAL

变化 CHANGES

物质产品的大规模生产使城市发生了革命性的变化，城市的发展脱离了原有的规划，超出了它本身的承受能力。

The large-scale production of materials brought about revolutionary changes in the development of cities. The urban expansion went beyond the existing planning and exceeded the capacity that the cities could bear.

大变革 REVOLUTIONARY

英国工程师伊桑巴德·金德姆·布鲁内尔（1806—1859）建造了桥梁、港口、铁路以及横跨大西洋的船只。当时，现代化工程建设工作比传统建筑工作更为重要。

Isambard Kingdom Brunel (1806-1859), a British engineer, constructed bridges, ports, railways, and even ships that crossed the Atlantic Ocean. At that time, engineering works were more important than architectural ones.

公共服务缺乏 LACK OF PUBLIC SERVICES

贫困的住宅区缺乏公共服务设施，比如下水道系统或饮用水系统。

Poor neighborhoods often lack public service facilities such as sewage or drinking water systems.

河流资源 RIVER RESOURCES

艾威尔河通航后，商船来往更加频繁。

After River Irwell was made navigable, commercial ships were able to travel more frequently.

污染 POLLUTION

工厂排放的黑烟，以及倾倒进河里或街道上的垃圾，严重污染着城市的环境。

The black smoke emitted by factories and the dumping of garbage into rivers and streets were severely polluting the urban environment.

照明设施不足
INSUFFICIENT LIGHTING

街道上的照明设施很少。只有少数灯柱上有一些油灯，光线非常昏暗。

There were very few lighting fixtures on the streets, with only a small number of oil lamps on some lamp posts, resulting in very dim lighting.

仓库 WAREHOUSES

原材料，包括棉花、烟草以及煤炭等，均存放在工厂之间的巨型工业建筑物中。

Raw materials, including cotton, tobacco, and coal, etc, were stored in giant industrial buildings located between factories.

无产阶级化 PROLETARIANIZATION

工人们不再独立工作，而是成为生产链中的环节。

Workers no longer worked independently, but became part of the production process.

工人阶级的住所
Working Class Housing

工业化进程为城市带来了越来越多的工厂和就业机会，促使农村人口迅速向城市迁移。在一些新的区域，工人负担得起的房屋激增，拥有成排房屋的住宅区也兴建起来。然而，这些住宅区所在区域大多贫困、脏乱，公共服务设施少得可怜，而且拥挤不堪。

The industrialization process brought more and more factories and job opportunities to cities, leading to a rapid migration of rural populations to urban areas. In some new regions, there was a surge in affordable housing for workers, and residential areas with rows of houses were also built. However, these residential areas were mostly located in impoverished, dirty, and crowded areas, with scarce public services.

阶级意识 CLASS-CONSCIOUSNESS

工人们的居住环境吵闹而拥挤。不同年龄的人挤在一起，分享各自的日常生活和不幸遭遇。据悉，这种拥挤的生活环境，正是工人紧密团结在一起的决定性因素之一。

The living environment of the workers was noisy and crowded. People of different ages were squeezed together, sharing their daily lives and unfortunate experiences. It was reported that this crowded living environment was one of the decisive factors that brought the workers together in close solidarity.

排屋① TERRACED HOUSE

排屋最大限度地利用了空间。有时候，人
们会将三排排屋连续建在一起。

Terraced houses made the most of space. Sometimes,
three rows of terraced houses were built together.

饮用水 DRINKING WATER

起初，工人阶级住宅区的房屋并没有建造室
内管道系统。饮用水需要从公共水源处获取。

In the beginning, there were no indoor plumbing systems
in the working class housing areas. Drinking water had
to be obtained from public water sources.

地下室 BASEMENT

地下室的房租相对便宜。有时候，会出现多个家
庭共同租住一个地下室的情况。

Renting a basement was relatively cheap, and sometimes
multiple families would share one basement as their living
space.

① 是住宅的一种式样，由多幢相连的双层或多层房屋组成，一排排屋之
内相邻的房屋共用同一堵墙。——译者注

你知道吗?
DID YOU KNOW?

一栋拥有40间房屋的楼房只有 **6** 个 **卫生间**。

A building with 40 rooms only had 6 toilets.

乡村住宅 RURAL HOUSING

在工业时代，乡村的住房同样很简陋，但不像城市里的房子那么拥挤。有的住宅区建有马厩、手工作业区和农场。家庭成员很多，大家共同分担日常工作。

In the industrial era, rural housing was also very simple, but not as crowded as houses in the city. Some residential areas were built with stables, handicraft areas, and farms. With many family members, everyone shared the daily work.

墙壁和屋顶 WALLS AND ROOFS

墙壁由红砖砌成，非常薄；屋顶由黑色或蓝色的石板瓦铺成。

Walls were made of thin red bricks, and roofs were covered with black or blue slate tiles.

阁楼 ATTICS

很小，而且并不是所有的房屋都有阁楼。有时候房主会把阁楼租给单身的工人。

The attics were small, and not all houses had them. Sometimes, the homeowners would rent out the attic to single workers.

顶楼 TOP FLOOR

已婚夫妇和他们的孩子们通常同住在顶楼的一间屋子里。

Married couples and their children typically shared one room on the top floor.

公共卫生间 PUBLIC TOILET

卫生间跟排屋相连，非常窄小。几个家庭共用一个卫生间。

The public toilet was connected to the terraced houses and was very narrow. Several families shared one toilet.

底层 GROUND FLOOR

底层只有一个房间，却"身兼数职"——厨房、客厅和餐厅。

The ground floor had only one room but served multiple functions as the kitchen, living room, and dining room.

利物浦与工业时代
Liverpool and the Industrial Age

19世纪下半叶，工业革命带来的影响不断扩大，迅速席卷了英国所有的城市和街道，也波及了其他国家。铁路网不断扩大，而且随着铁路的出现，城市景观也随之发生变化。火车站的兴建，更是带来了强烈的冲击——宾馆建起来了，咖啡厅和商店激增，街道变得嘈杂、繁忙，呈现出一派现代生活的景象。

In the second half of the 19th century, the impact of the Industrial Revolution continued to expand, rapidly sweeping through all cities and streets in Britain and affecting other countries as well. The railway network continued to expand, and with the appearance of railways, the urban landscape also changed. The construction of railway stations brought about a strong impact—hotels were built, coffee shops and stores increased rapidly, and the streets became noisy and busy, presenting a scene of modern life.

利物浦的发展 THE GROWTH OF LIVERPOOL

利物浦于1207年建立，起初还只是一个小镇，直到1880年才发展成为城市。18世纪，因为拥有海港的优势，利物浦发展迅速。到了19世纪，40%的航运贸易都经过利物浦港口，给这个城市带来了巨大的经济扩张，这一点从令人印象深刻的建筑上就可以看出来。

Liverpool was founded in 1207 as a small town and only became a city in 1880. Its rapid development in the 18th century was due to its advantage as a seaport. By the 19th century, 40% of shipping trade passed through Liverpool's port, bringing enormous economic expansion to the city, as evident in its impressive architecture.

位置 LOCATION

车站和港口是构建城市经济生活的两条轴线。

The station and the port were the two axes that shaped urban economic life.

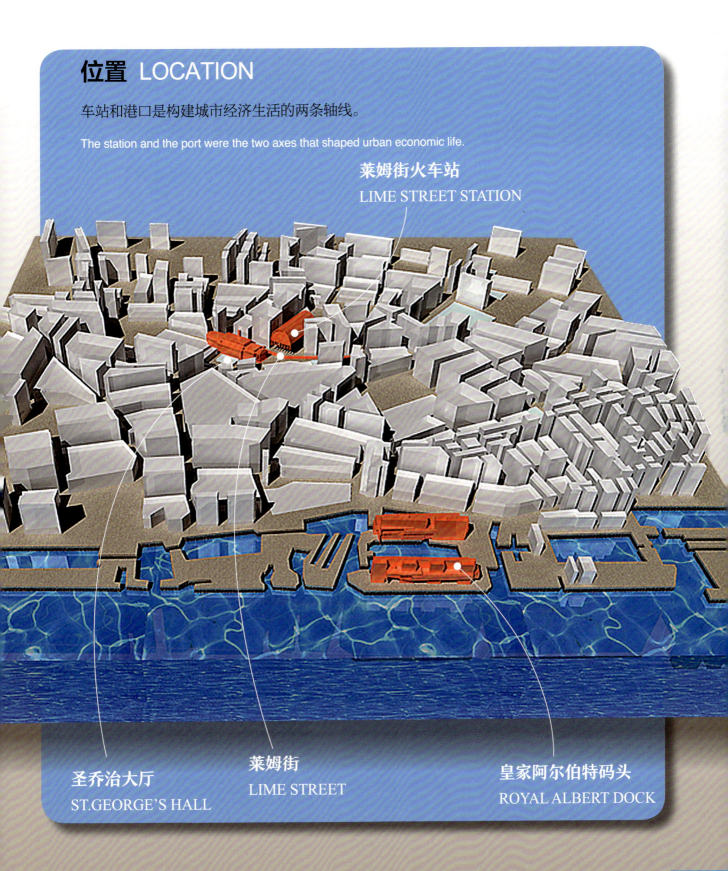

莱姆街火车站
LIME STREET STATION

圣乔治大厅
ST.GEORGE'S HALL

莱姆街
LIME STREET

皇家阿尔伯特码头
ROYAL ALBERT DOCK

第二城市 SECOND CITY

利物浦虽然比伦敦富有，但从重要性上来说，是英国排名第二的城市。

Liverpool was wealthier than London, but in terms of importance, it was ranked second after London.

酒吧 THE PUBS

在莱姆街，你会看到许多酒吧，比如皇冠酒吧（第一家酒吧，1859年开业）和葡萄藤酒吧。

Along Lime Street are many pubs, such as the Crown (the first pub, which opened in 1859) and the Vine.

莱姆街 LIME STREET

修建于1790年，是城市转型的象征。

Lime Street was built in 1790 and was a symbol of urban transformation.

旅馆 THE HOTEL

西北酒店建于1871年，主要为乘坐火车的旅客提供住宿。

The North Western Hotel was built in 1871 and mainly provided accommodation for passengers traveling by train.

圣乔治大厅 ST.GEORGE'S HALL

圣乔治大厅是一座极为壮观的建筑，里面还建有法庭，厅前广场的对面是火车站和西北酒店。

St George's Hall is a magnificent building that houses a court inside. Across the square in front of the hall are the railway station and the North Western Hotel.

先锋城市 PIONEER CITY

作为重要的航运港口，利物浦在许多领域都占据了领先地位，这一点从港口和铁路线就可以看出来，而这些都是城市高速发展的主要推动力。

As an important shipping port, Liverpool held a leading position in many fields, as evidenced by its port and railway lines, which were the main driving forces behind the city's rapid development.

港口 THE PORT

托马斯·斯蒂尔斯码头是世界上第一个拥有商业浮船坞的港口。

Thomas Steers Quay was the first port in the world to have a commercial wet dock.

火车站

THE RAILWAY STATION

莱姆街火车站于1833年开始修建，1836年建成。利物浦和曼彻斯特是最早由铁路线连接起来的城市。

The construction of Lime Street station began in 1833 and was completed in 1836. Liverpool and Manchester were the first cities to be connected by a railway line.

杂乱的交通 CHAOTIC TRAFFIC

莱姆街非常繁忙，除了私人马车，还有载客马车——一种马拉的公共汽车，在街上来来往往。

Lime Street was very busy, with not only private carriages but also hackney carriages—a type of horse-drawn public transportation, going back and forth on the street.

资产阶级的住所
Bourgeois Housing

　　19世纪末，资产阶级的力量开始在欧洲主要城市崛起。他们住在彰显各自经济成就的小楼里，每栋小楼都有几层高。作为楼房的主人，他们一般住在二楼——整栋楼中最便利、最敞亮、最通风的一层。剩下的房间出租给第三方或者供仆人居住。资产阶级住宅中这种特色鲜明的分配方式反映了统治资本主义社会的秩序和逻辑。

At the end of the 19th century, the power of the bourgeoisie began to rise in major European cities. They lived in small buildings that showcased their economic achievements, each building was several stories high. As the owners of the building, they generally lived on the first floor—the most convenient, brightest and most ventilated floor in the entire building. The remaining rooms were rented to third parties or used for servants to live in. This distinctive allocation of living space in bourgeois residences reflected the order and logic that ruled the capitalist society.

对比 COMPARISON

为了彰显自己优人一等的地位，资产阶级用最优质的材料装潢他们的住宅，试图让其他居民区黯然失色。

To showcase their superior status, the bourgeoisie decorated their homes with the top-quality materials, attempting to make other residential areas pale in comparison.

观察建筑物
OBSERVING THE BUILDING

多层的楼房是社会进步与经济增长的象征。在人口密集的城镇，不同阶层间的社会经济差距变得越来越明显。

Multi-story buildings were a symbol of social progress and economic growth. In densely populated urban areas, the socioeconomic gap between different classes became increasingly evident.

彰显身份
CONVEY WEALTH AND STATUS

房主常常在入口处摆放各种装饰品、时尚的家具、小型画作和雕塑。另外，这里也是连接所有楼层的主楼梯的所在之处。

Homeowners often placed various decorations, trendy furniture, small paintings, and sculptures at the entrance. This was also where the main staircase connecting all floors was located.

底层 GROUND FLOOR

底层一般不住人，这里的大门面向街道，没有私密性。

大多数楼房在底层设有门店，属于家族业务，面向街道，对外开放。

The ground floor was generally not used for living, because its entrance faced the street, lacking privacy.
Most of the buildings had stores on the ground floor, which belonged to family businesses. They faced the street, and were open to the public.

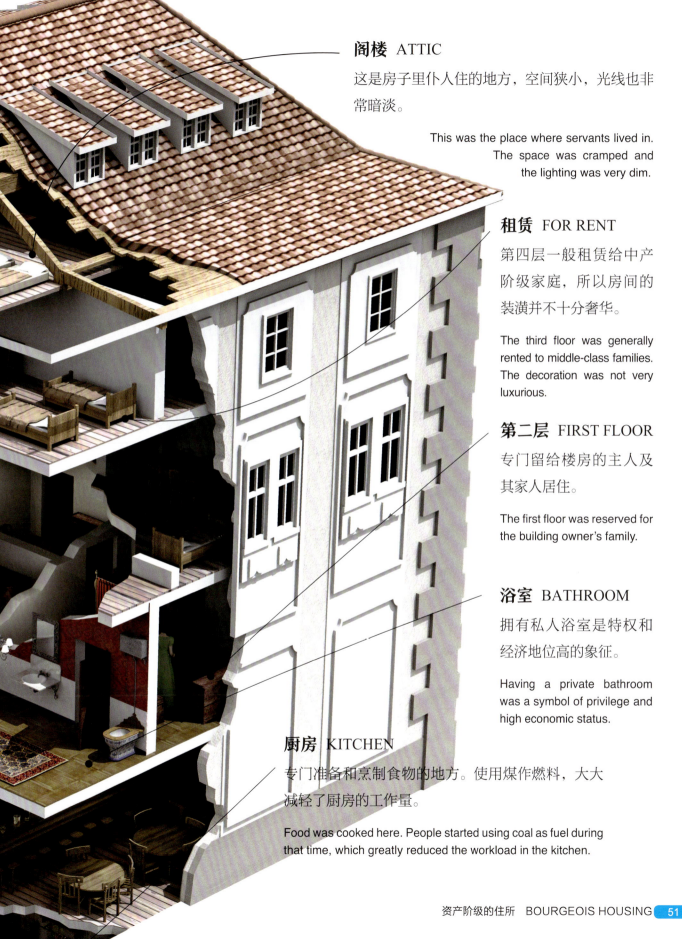

阁楼 ATTIC

这是房子里仆人住的地方，空间狭小，光线也非常暗淡。

This was the place where servants lived in. The space was cramped and the lighting was very dim.

租赁 FOR RENT

第四层一般租赁给中产阶级家庭，所以房间的装潢并不十分奢华。

The third floor was generally rented to middle-class families. The decoration was not very luxurious.

第二层 FIRST FLOOR

专门留给楼房的主人及其家人居住。

The first floor was reserved for the building owner's family.

浴室 BATHROOM

拥有私人浴室是特权和经济地位高的象征。

Having a private bathroom was a symbol of privilege and high economic status.

厨房 KITCHEN

专门准备和烹制食物的地方。使用煤作燃料，大大减轻了厨房的工作量。

Food was cooked here. People started using coal as fuel during that time, which greatly reduced the workload in the kitchen.

火车与铁路
Train and Railway

1830年，"火箭号"蒸汽机车举行了通车仪式，宣告英国第一条铁路线正式开通。19世纪，铁路运输持续发展，连接了欧洲的各个角落，成为了经济增长和社会变革的重要推动力。

In 1830, the steam locomotive "Rocket" held its inaugural ceremony, marking the official opening of the first railway line in Britain. Throughout the 19th century, railway transportation continued to develop, connecting every corner of Europe. It became a significant driver of economic growth and social transformation.

储蓄槽 TANKS

与车头相连，用来储水和煤炭的小车厢。

A small wagon carrying water and coal was attached to the train.

钢铁业大爆发
IRON AND STEEL BOOM

蒸汽机的制造和数千千米铁轨的铺设导致对钢铁的巨大需求。钢铁业一发不可收拾，一跃成为19世纪最赚钱的行业之一。

The construction of steam engines and the laying of thousands of kilometers of railway created a spectacular demand for iron and steel. The steel industry experienced an expansion that made it one of the most profitable businesses of the 19th century.

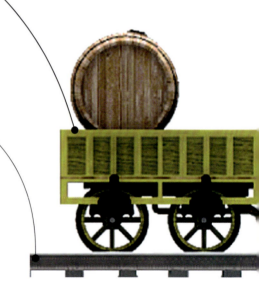

蒸汽 THE STEAM

燃烧煤产生蒸汽，蒸汽的压力作用于活塞，活塞通过连杆推动火车轮子转动。

Coal was burned to produce steam. The pressure of the steam moved the piston, which acted on the wheels of the locomotive via connecting rods.

通风系统 DRAUGHT SYSTEM

让蒸汽从锅炉的管道系统排出，并通过通风口吸入大量的氧气，帮助燃烧，从而加热锅炉里的水。

Allowed steam to escape through pipes from the boiler and created a strong intake of oxygen through the vent, facilitating the combustion process and thus heating the water.

驱动轮
DRIVE WHEEL

你知道吗?

DID YOU KNOW?

1830 年 9 月 15 日首次试运行时，"火箭号"的速度为 **47** 千米 / 时。

On September 15, 1830, during the trial run, the speed of the "Rocket" was 47 kilometers per hour.

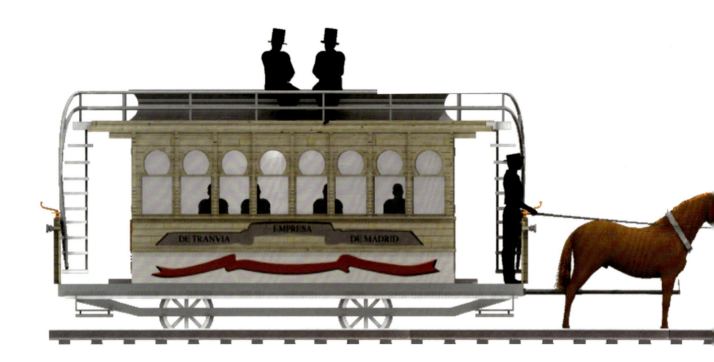

铁路普及 POPULARIZATION OF RAILWAY TRIP

19世纪后期，乘坐火车出行已经成为日常生活的一部分，铁路线把城市、乡村和港口通通连接了起来。

In the late 19th century, taking a train trip had become a part of daily life, as railway lines connected cities, towns, and ports together.

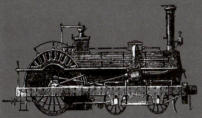

19世纪40年代　1840S

经过10年的优化改良，蒸汽机的制造材料几乎全部变成了钢铁。增加新的轮轴以提高牵引力之后，载货蒸汽机车的平均速度达到每小时30—40千米。

After a decade of optimization and improvement, almost all steam engines were made of steel. New axles were added to increase traction, and the average speed of freight steam locomotives reached 30-40 kilometers per hour.

19世纪80年代　1880S

在这10年中，美国和德国都开始致力于研究电力——20世纪广泛使用的能源。

During these 10 years, both the United States and Germany began to focus on researching electricity—an energy source that would become widely used in the 20th century.

16—19世纪
FROM THE 16TH TO THE 19TH CENTURY

从16世纪开始，小货车就被用于矿山，一般由人力或马匹拉动，在木质轨道上行驶。第一条供载客马车通行的铁路线路出现于19世纪。

Since the 16th century, wagons mounted on wooden rails and pulled by horses or men were used in mines. The first railroad lines for passengers with wagons pulled by horses appeared in the 19th century.

工厂式学校
Factory-Style Schools

18世纪，资本主义通过制造业霸权得到巩固。工业革命也由此开启了各个方面的变革，比如社会和经济结构、工厂、工人阶级、城市发展、新兴能源、大规模生产以及工作日和工会条例，这些都是这一时代的标志。

In the 18th century, capitalism was solidified through the hegemony of manufacturing. The Industrial Revolution thus ignited transformations in various aspects, such as social and economic structures, factories, the working class, urban development, emerging energy, mass production, and regulations on working days and trade unions, all of which were hallmarks of this era.

同质性和纪律性
HOMOGENEITY AND DISCIPLINE

1798年，约瑟夫·兰开斯特在英国创立了一所学校。整个校区只有一间没有任何分隔的教室，1 000名学生坐在一起，由老师统一授课。天赋较高的学生负责把老师讲授的内容解释给其他同学。所有的学生根据科目被分为十个小组，不分年龄。这种教学模式与工厂的制度非常相似。

In 1798, Joseph Lancaster founded a school in Britain. The entire campus consisted of a single classroom with no partitions, where 1, 000 students sat together and were taught by a single teacher. More gifted students were responsible for explaining the teacher's material to the rest of the class. All students, regardless of age, were divided into ten small groups based on subject. This teaching model was very similar to the factory system.

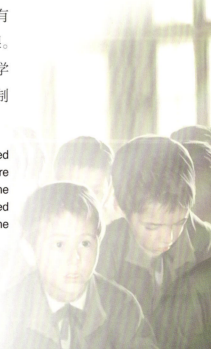

教师 TEACHER

通过大喊、拍手、铃声或手势来给出指令，然后由辅导员解释并传达给学生们。

The teacher gave instructions by shouting, clapping, ringing or gesturing, which were then interpreted by the tutor and passed on to the students.

等级制度 HIERARCHY

学生们在教室里所坐的位置代表了他们的地位，最聪明的学生往往离教师最近。

Where students sat in the classroom reflected their status, with the brightest students tending to sit closest to the teacher.

读、写、算术和宗教
READING, WRITING, MATHS AND RELIGION

不同学科的课程一般同时进行：一个小组在沙桌上练习写字，另一个小组在做有关银行的练习，第三个小组面对墙上的海报练习朗读。

Courses in different subjects generally proceeded concurrently: one group practiced writing at the sand table, another group worked on exercises related to banking, and a third group practiced reading aloud in front of posters on the wall.

辅导员 TUTORS

通常由一些比较聪明的学生担任，他们负责把知识传递给特定的小组成员。

Tutors were usually taken up by some of the smarter students, who were responsible for imparting knowledge to specific group members.

授课 TEACHING

教师站在讲台后面给学生讲课。

The teacher stood behind the podium lecturing to the students.

学习阅读
LEARNING TO READ

学生们最先学习的是字母，然后是音节，最后才是字词和句子。

The students first learned the alphabet, then syllables, and finally words and sentences.

授课方法
TEACHING METHODS

教师先口述知识点，再让学生重复和背诵。

The teacher first verbally presented the knowledge, then had the students repeat and recite them.

课前准备 PREPARATION

上课前，每位辅导员都会接到当天的指令。

Before class, each tutor would receive the instructions for the day.

学生 STUDENTS

每十人一组，接受某一门学科的指导，然后轮换另外一个小组接受指导。

Students were grouped in tens, receiving guidance in one subject, and then rotated to another group for further instruction.

术语及专有名词 | Names and Terms

艾威尔河 River Irwell

奥斯曼男爵 Baron Haussmann

巴黎 Paris

布里奇沃特运河 Bridgewater Canal

产业工人 industrial workers

德国 Germany

等级制度 hierarchy

恩格斯 Engels

法国 France

法兰西第二帝国 The Second French Empire

纺纱机 spinners

飞梭 flying shuttle

弗雷德里克·泰勒 Frederick Taylor

（芝加哥）干草市场惨案 Haymarket affair

工业革命 Industrial Revolution

工业化 industrialization

工业资本主义 industrial capitalism

共产党宣言 Communist Manifesto

股份 shares

皇家阿尔伯特码头 Royal Albert Dock

经济学家 economist

卡尔·马克思 Karl Marx

莱姆街 Lime Street

莱姆街火车站 Lime Street Station

里沃利路 Rue de Rivoli

历史学家 historian

利物浦 Liverpool

罗奇代尔运河 Rochdale Canal

曼彻斯特 Manchester

美国 The United States

欧洲 Europe

驱动轮 drive wheel

绕线机 winding machines

塞瓦斯托波尔大道 Boulevard de Sébastopol

沙特莱广场 Place du Châtelet

社会学家 sociologist

社会主义者 socialist

圣米歇尔大道 Boulevard Saint-Michel

圣乔治大厅 St.George's Hall

梳棉机 carding machines

水轮 water wheel

泰勒主义 Taylorism

托马斯·斯蒂尔斯码头 Thomas Steers Quay

万国邮政联盟 The Universal Postal Union

维多利亚站 Victoria Station

无产阶级 proletariat

无政府主义者 anarchist

宪章运动 Chartism

亚当·斯密 Adam Smith

伊莱·惠特尼 Eli Whitney

伊桑巴德·金德姆·布鲁内尔 Isambard
    Kingdom Brunel

英国 Britain

约瑟夫·兰开斯特 Joseph Lancaster

约瑟夫·玛丽·雅卡尔 Joseph Marie Jacquard

詹姆斯·瓦特 James Watt

珍妮纺纱机 Spinning Jenny

蒸汽机 steam engine

殖民主义 colonialism

图书在版编目（CIP）数据

小机器　大进步：中英双语给孩子讲工业革命：汉、英 / 懿海文化著、绘；刘丽丽译 . -- 北京：科学普及出版社，2023.8
ISBN 978-7-110-10579-5

Ⅰ．①小… Ⅱ．①懿… ②刘… Ⅲ．①产业革命—少儿读物—汉、英 Ⅳ．① F419-49

中国国家版本馆 CIP 数据核字（2023）第 061726 号

策划编辑：李世梅　马跃华		封面设计：巫　粲	
责任编辑：张　惠		责任校对：张晓莉	
助理编辑：林晓萌		责任印制：马宇晨	
版式设计：蚂蚁设计			

出版：科学普及出版社　　　　　　　　　　　　　　邮编：100081
发行：中国科学技术出版社有限公司发行部　　　发行电话：010-62173865
地址：北京市海淀区中关村南大街 16 号　　　　　传真：010-62173081
网址：http://www.cspbooks.com.cn

开本：889mm×1194mm　　1/16　　　印刷：北京顶佳世纪印刷有限公司
印张：4.25　　　　　　　　　　　　　　　　　字数：90 千字
版次：2023 年 8 月第 1 版　　　　　　　　　印次：2023 年 8 月第 1 次印刷

书号：ISBN 978-7-110-10579-5 / F·274　　　　定价：68.00 元

（凡购买本社图书，如有缺页、倒页、脱页者，本社发行部负责调换）